D0462260

QUESTIONS IN BED

STEWART COLE

icehouse poetry
an imprint of Goose Lane Editions

Edited by James Langer.
Cover image detailed from "Police Lights" by Yume Ninja, deviantart.com.
Cover and page design by Julie Scriver.
Printed in Canada.
10 9 8 7 6 5 4 3 2 1

Library and Archives Canada Cataloguing in Publication

Cole, Stewart, 1978-
        Questions in bed / Stewart Cole.

Poems.
ISBN 978-0-86492-684-5

        I. Title.

PS8605.O439Q48 2012   C811'.6   C2012-902944-0

Goose Lane Editions acknowledges the generous support of the Canada Council for the Arts, the Government of Canada through the Canada Book Fund (CBF), and the Government of New Brunswick through the Department of Culture, Tourism, and Healthy Living.

Goose Lane Editions
500 Beaverbrook Court, Suite 330
Fredericton, New Brunswick
CANADA E3B 5X4
www.gooselane.com

CONTENTS

To those who lie awake

Beware of anonymous letters — you may have written them,
in a wordless implosion of sleep.
— John Ashbery

MERMAN

Mornings he emerges from beyond the slick drape,
shedding drops and peals of steam, phasing in

to a prison of porcelain and chrome
as if being undreamed, slowly reclaimed

by clean lines of manhood. Once out
he winds the towel around his metamorphosed half,

the dark undercontinent of his origins
already sinking back into fantasy.

Unfogging the mirror to watch himself stand,
he scrapes the algae from his jaw

believing it stubble, having let sink away,
like a penny tossed into something bottomless,

the message he bore from the deeps
for his surface self, at which now I

can only conjecture. A melt warning,
a vengeful cry from the fomenting dumpsite,

an update on the status of dead ancestors?
Or something in a figurative code aimed

specifically at me, e.g., "The anglerfish
patrols the seabottom like a vicious conscience..."

I am guilty of feeling absolved by sleep
without ever thinking closely about what from,

what inner criminal's lungs fill with ink and ether
each time I go under. Whether what gulps up

to daylight is man, or myth, or monster.

INVERTING THE BIRDS

They teeter like the casually employed:
along the highway's brackish ditches up
the river valley slanting into Ottawa,
red-winged blackbirds metronome
atop the reed-stalks in crooked rows
that their matching flashes make appear
patterned. The metropole commute
continues apace, glinting into meanwhile,
with even eighteen-wheelers taking on
the anonymity of sedans. Those of us
with steady jobs will get to them,
unless this fiscal season's cross-lane
audit falls to one of our accounts,
spitting gas receipts from the glovebox
and unstalking slashes of upward love.

Black-winged redbirds live among us,
relentlessly symbolic because colourful
and rare. Next to imaginary, they slip through
the papered cracks in some way opposite
the jobless. Lacking private hells,
they cheep to one another, bound
as birds. My *Peterson's* will affirm them
as tanagers until the day it burns, by which time
many duplicates will have been produced
to teach and delude us. Suppose I saw one right
now, as I speed along, playing clock
among its cousins, their doppelgänger, wrought
of scarlet luck. Might not a second split in which
I hate and love this life at once? At twice?

A REBUTTAL

> Money talks.
> — *North American proverb*

Adorned with purse-lipped busts
of power brokers cashed-out
long enough to gild their deficits
and liquefy their minted mugs
among the public trust, it keeps
hush. Depends on chronic mass
amnesia for its thrust, the way
a case too long before the judge
finds its column-inches nipped
away at like a small inheritance
from a spinster aunt. It persists
in retailing the spent myth
of that shoot-second cowpoke
Loquacious Cash, yet gloves
our eager faces like a count
affronted when we dare demand
it speak up or repeat itself.
                                At best
its grubby riffle can approximate
a lulling susurration, a comforting
motherless shush. At worst
a hiss rent from a snake's larynx,
viciously post-Edenic. Most
often though, it occupies
a sonic shelf shared (grudgingly
no doubt) with tapped keys
and swept verandahs, cleared
throats and muffled traffic heard
through layered plexi-panes
many success-storeys above
the street: extraverbal crumbs
we sometimes hear silting off

the edges of our aspirates. Cash —
do you hear that? — says zilch,
just lies basking in the taxed
unfilled silence after every
inarticulate cha-ching.

1-1-9

I squint back at the hotel from the beach;
its neocolonial façade cancels
a view of anything but itself, its cream
stucco immensity. Except it isn't

a façade. We build Babylons, funtime
garrisons against the waves furling in
from all angles—the erosive sea, seething
locals, this region's pleasure-weapon

the sun. Under shadow of a grass umbrella
at midday I wonder very little,
numbed by knowing this a place a poet risks
decommission for even admitting

having been. Dry with shame, I wade in
and order a Mai-Tai, tipping a damp
American dollar as we all do, despite
our all-inclusive wristbands and no matter

our nationality. Lingua franca Washingtonia.
Yesterday Denisha, one of the activities girls,
pointed out to me the pendulous drupes
of unripe sea grapes, clustered rows

of chlorophyll orbs just beginning
to sugar into purple. Six dawns a week
at the crack of her fourteen-hour shift
she spectres the strand to pluck

any ready ones. Of course I asked
my tongue's question, to which she replied:
Sweet but still bitter, and with a very large pit—
which makes sense from trees that gnarl up

from hourglass spillage. Now I'm lying
three rums deep, otter-floating
with a fourth perched on my sternum,
looking up from the shallows at a vast sky

portentous with frigatebirds, their tails forked
like implements of torture. A dread
lingers: that one may swoop down
and effect its dark piracy

upon my touristic soul. With such a range
of poisons at my command, how to commit
to just one? The chambermaid refills
my minifridge daily with Carib — a beer

that steals its name from a native
Antillean people and their extinct
language. I drink it because it's there,
the blue-and-sunburst cans slick with cold

inverse of sweat, soothing my afternoon
forehead apulse with the facepalms
of the Sun God sloughed-off with cane liquor,
to which the candied corn-soda taste

after the crack and hiss provides a welcome,
if ill-advised, contrast. It calls to me.
At this point in the day I'm beatific
with guilt, like one who gluttons himself

until he comes out the other side starving. Up
the beach, along the fleshly poolside past
the families idling at the shut door of the all-
you-can-eat, along the unjungled paths

through palm, banana, and traveller's tree
to the airy foyer, where when I order
a Blue Hawaii to take back to my room,
the tuxedoed bartender I shit you not answers,

Ya mon. I duly George him, and mount
the marble staircase to what the situation demands
I call my domicile, collapsing
to mattress. After zoning out a spell

I sit up for a sip and notice the red-lettered
sticker on the phone, faded to symbolize
its advice being so rarely heeded here:
IN CASE OF EMERGENCY DIAL 1-1-9.

1-1-9! *Hello? Yes this is a re-*
verse emergency. I've resorted
to vacating the moral north. My sister
is getting married. I'm giving her

away. I see myself as if from the sand up,
callus-soled, politely slavering, essentially
a Babylonian. A baby-man alone amid
a Babylon demanding to be chanted down.

SIRENS

They no longer tempt. Instead
they omen us, tear hysteric holes
in the linen of awareness, vacate
the daylit zones between our ribs,
momentarily blare us airless.

Main Street's heavy pulse falls faint
beneath their shrieks as they wend among
the traffic clots. They pull taut the drumskin
of the collective ear, needling eyelets
through which inky wisps thread to mind.

A dark ache in the temples;
jaw grinds shut like door of cloister,
hairshirting thought. Their shrillness peaks
as finally they speed by in strobes
of too-bright blood and a blue of veins

drained of O_2. Which of course
isn't true. By discomfort's woozy
torchlight I remind myself they wail
not to remind us how near the lives
made worse they scream towards can be,

but to help. My temptation
is to steal the future for myself,
even if it blows up in my hand
like an acme bomb. Reminder:
most times our ears are plugged for us.

WEED 'EM AND REAP

The first night Fall feels like its namesake, I
do my sanity the doubtful kindness
of a twilight walk. Headphoned anonymity
suits me to the dark like a zippered fleece,
as warm synths and beats hum a home for me
amid what marks of exile I can't ignore:
the traffic snarls and strains rottweilerly
at every painted line it pauses for;

pedestrians are few. But in this blitz
of music hissed into by muted civic
stimuli — whispers of speed, guttered leaves,
prongs of skyless light — I refuse to miss
the country, golden and oblivious
and hunkered out there harvesting our needs.

But still its analog static bleeds up through
my digital fidelity to Now,
a spectral gospel splicing my techno
into shards of undanceable bad news.
And still I refuse: slough off the shockwave
of nostalgia, cling to urbanity
and grit against the bunk epiphany
that threatens to make me its wistful slave —

the one that goes something like this: *Yon vast*
italicized landscape that lies beyond
the concrete verges, verdancy that yawns
like a forever-infant god at all
horizons, heightless tree from which we fall
and blissful verblessness to which at last...

This postcard fiction duly appoints me
its speaker. Its appeal resides in how
it makes a lack of shelter gleam like home,
like nakedness's faith in the power
of the callus, the coal-walker's thirst
for unfelt pain. This postcard's friction rubs
the parts of me that bear the city worst,
gravelling me down to sensile hubs:

these urgency-anticipating ears,
bleeding vigilance; the matter in-between
that needs to mortalize the sirened air,
phantomiming tragic scenes unseen;
and bruised, my evil-sided shoulder, where
a tiny mythic creature roosts and sneers:

"Grow yourself. Own your choice
to light out from valley-home
as what it was: a boy convinced
of more love owed him
yet dumb to knowing how poor
is so much of what trombones
itself as such. Bad jazz
destined for empty lifts or ringtones,
sad and lonely-making face
and body collage. Boo hooey.
Home yourself. Ungroan and stoop
down to what's chosen you
to choose it: a life of clues,
of undidactic lessons
and mostly absent wounds
you probe regardless, in the hope
of one day minding gold,
of yes's full eclipse
across that dark, persistent — "

QUESTIONS IN BED

I wonder who's at risk to lose themselves
tonight, who fears or should

the long pall of schism
natural dark brings with it? To what act

or happening do those amped sirens fling
their ululations? What newly phantom-damp

patch of pavement hearkens their despatch?
Was it someone's out-

of-character axe-frenzy? Am I next?
If just above my breath I whisper *fire* —

could that help? Do they sound to you
like they're getting closer,

faintly loudening like succubi
scenting male fear? I fail to tell my birds

apart anymore — are they cops, ambulance,
or some emergent reaper-response team

like ghostbusters? Isn't urgency an egg
always spawning new crack squads?

Tell me, are these questions careening off
the ceiling with any force?

Or is there someone upstairs at least,
absorbing them through itchy feet?

CHASE SEQUENCE

1. Proem: How It Must End

The shift of evasive shoulder blades undershirt,
the glint of the receding bumper in the sun,
the license plate numbers fading like a trip
      down the eye chart,
the tip of the tail as it slips at last into the bush,
the polka-dotted monster laughing out its heart
from its hiding place, escaped from me again.

Born to learn to wear loss with winningness,
to smile and shake my wishful head,
jostling my skull-bound wishes like standers on a lurching train
      who quickly straighten,
undeterred from their destinations. Born to learn not to navigate,
but to be drawn, pulled toward the ever-magnetic north
of forward, the vanishing slit in the morrow.

Post-religious, but spiritual because who isn't,
I prove my devotion by chasing it like a tail,
chasing and escaping faith, a game of stripes and tigers,
      catch as catch can't.
This motion proves me by pursuit: daily without fail
I spy it lurking in ambush, wearing a mask of me.
We chase therefore we flee therefore we can't not be.

It's a sapphic rom-com we inhabit, a sweetbitter love-in
destined to end at the valley's summit, to climax
in the moments just after our gasping quarry slumps back and sighs,
      "I think we've lost them" —
and then they let their eyes neglect the mirrors and relax
just long enough for us to drench them in our headlights
before their urgent engine revs them gone,

deliciously gone. After their escape the air
will throb with the steady slowing of pulses, ours and theirs
and even those of the imagined audience always in vicarious pursuit
       (impossible love)
as they watch, the air will hang heavy as a bronze bell
left unrung, and every lung in airshot will swell
and fill, their bodies both scared and desperate to move.

2. *Ahistoric Man*

To hunt for food and strike for flame
and inhabit the skins of kill
became the basic human skills
at some point between the descent
and the building of towns with names,
before the games of government
but after the straying of will
toward windows of adornment,
around the time the toxins came.

When suddenly love wasn't thighs
and meat didn't have to be charred
and life didn't have to be hard,
at least always, when now and then
we could slip through roomfuls of friends
having downed five glassfuls of stars
and light at last on the backyard,
navigating tiki torch fires
to drink in one another's eyes.

Starring everyone. There's a calm
one detects in reproductions
of ancient hunting expeditions,
the jaws and eyes of men intent
in knowing that the only balm
for hunger is alive, a scent
they track beyond intoxication
to full stomachs and humble tents,
the sated body's silent psalms.

Is our sapience a measure
of our insatiability,
or in mere decades will it be
revealed that everything we chased,
every empty chest we treasured
for golden hearts that never raced
outstripped our human pedigree,
attuned our tongues to fewer tastes,
and museum-cased our pleasures?

I don't always want what I chase.
The skin of women gives me clues.
My heritage forbids the blues.
The Protestant Work Ethic sucks.
I'm lashing out with my embrace,
hoping hard to soften luck.
The best ideas leave a bruise,
said the comet as it struck —
I'm digging up a better place.

3. *Spermatazoom*

To be the only one of millions loosed,
unleashed like microscopic bloodhounds
to sniff out a missing child yet unborn,
a pack of amniotic plague-dogs wrought
of mucile pre-blood and un-flesh imbued
with blueprints enough to help set a-tick
a tiny life-bomb.
           To be the only one:
this wish begins before the swimming seed
embeds its eyeless head, a soft harpoon
shot down the rose canal of soon-to-be
in wet pursuit of a target so still
and yet so hard to find it comes to seem
holy, or at least immersed in mystery
at depths reserved for treasure or monster.
And so the wish for exclusivity begins,
with millions of us driven onward by it,
the same wish multitudinous Whitman
declaimed along the broad-lined avenues
of his nation-poem:
                O to propagate
until the very lawns spring from our seed
and grass grows tinted in the tones of flesh
and every drop of dew on every blade
reflects a navel-gazing human face,
agape in the utopia of Us.
                  We are
because the swimming wish cannot conceive
of any aim beyond continuance,
because success consists of anti-death,
of staving expiration off until
the lucky reach the life at tunnel's end,
and being born we instantly forget
how our ecto-fathers have by now chased
enough for a lifetime, and therefore we
begin, propelled by only spindly legs
toward the pre-remembrance of a swim.

4. Kindergardening

It wasn't about our parents' plants, but what hid
in handfuls of soil and on the underlips of leaves,
what we might encase under punctured lid,
what small abominations we might teach them to believe.

But they'd seen too much of course, witnessed love
and divorce, abuse of drugs and mothers torn
between today and the life above:
at moments they'd even considered not having been born.

So our sowbugs and millipedes could not adulterate
their calm as they worked, weeding with strained rumps
around tomatoes and beets planted too late
in the busy spring to attain their fullest plump,

but planted all the same. When we would tug their shirts
to show them what we'd herded out from under rocks —
the silver wormy-shelled excrecences of dirt —
they never failed to fail at feigning shock.

Impossible to show, our disappointment,
kept inside, only drove us, like little Fausts, to more voraciously pursue
the infinitude of tiny demons in the ointment
that greased the lenses that we saw the garden through.

We boldly jarred wolf spiders, farmed red ants,
antagonized stag beetles until their frantic pincers clacked
like scythes of ice against the glass, suffered pinches on our hands
that jolted us from the dream of family into fact:

the morning we awoke to find the green mantis dead,
decapitated, and the white one, her thorax fat with spawn,
dispassionately toying with the severed head,
we somehow knew our parents had finally gone.

We think of finding them still, though jaded out
of needing them to gasp at every creature
as we did, until the hard years without them left no doubt:
the vacant garden is the children's decreator.

5. *The Metamorphs*

And then their bodies change:
for years unwittingly in bud
they wake with swollen throats
or hips or shoulders, full
of suddenly explicit spunk
enough to conquer this,

this common cold-blooded world
for which no living cure —
beyond a never-breaking heat
unto delirium,
a dizzyness impossible
to think within — exists.

And so their bodies change:
this one grows a prophet's beard,
a hooded mask of manginess
that hides his pimply cheeks
and authorizes him
to be ignored at street corners;

this other one absents herself so
completely into fantasy
she thins, and seems unplugged,
as though half of what she takes in
is feeding astral selves on planes
only reachable by drugs.

In Ovid maybe they'd have changed
into trees or constellations,
escaping rape by gods
through spontaneous mutation,
confounding the economy
of orifice and skin;

but now the most horrific parts
of pubescence happen within,
inchoate frustrations
that fall like purple dusk
on lunar hearts doomed in wanting just—
but not *only*—bodily love.

6. Interlude: Mute Swans Sing

Having scummed our habitats,
confined us to parks,
commandeered us bodily
for sundry artworks—

What of our innocence survives
your oppositional thumbs?
A clump of feathers sullied in a fist,
a clutch of windy poems.

You eulogize our nobility
yet mingle as we melt,
shaping fountains and napkins after us:
great unstainers of guilt.

We refuse to play the white to your wrongs
any longer. This is a protest song.

Millennia we've given our necks
epitomizing grace,
the sexually flexible
and the unbending chaste.

You're ill? We're medicinal,
a sentimental pill
ground and droppered in the dewy eye
to ivory your pale.

What you're after can't be caught
in flagrante or a net:
your humanity confounds
progréss with profligate.

We refuse to play the white to your wrongs
any longer. This is a protest song.

7. *Hooky*

Days when sunshine won't take *no*
I simply can't for an answer get rare,
and next thing you've got obligations up
the yin-yang, tipped balance sheets
without a wind to throw them to.

Hooking-off never seemed so complicated,
sociological: closing books
to burn the noonday coner at a single end,
pontificate in turn on the virtues
of rock, roll another one, flip the tape
back to side A. What I wouldn't do.

To the ever-growing list of what I wouldn't do
for kicks, danger, or simply to forget,
one might now add most illegal drugs,
speeding cars, tripping out
to hooky licks on tinny tape-decks,
or any combination thereof. It pains me
to admit my experimental days
have faded to hypotheses,
as inconclusive as the long-term
safety of GM foods.

I exaggerate. It doesn't pain me any more
than subtle ever-rising liquor taxes do,
a pinching in the pocket gotten over quicker
than *achoo*, a sickness unexpressed
in any symptom other than the odd
paroxysm of wistfulness

and wishing it otherwise: 'Is it true,
has my discontent collapsed under the elephantine
banality of rebellion? Am I flat and happy,
or simply well-adjusted, overschooled
in achy mornings after ditching math?'

8. *The Answer of Travel*

> Should we have stayed at home and thought of here?
> —*Elizabeth Bishop*

There are too many minarets to have imagined,
all roofed with green tiles topped
with a skewer of gold balls, a uniformity
that makes it almost easy to believe
all point to one God. The skyline seems to reject
whatever geometry the onlooker's mind wants
to impose on its pre-dentistry underbite;
its stucco teeth jut lopsidedly;
we marvel at its botched orthotecture
until the call to prayer jars us awestruck.

However temporarily, God yawns
open to our diagnosticism, our keen minds
sifting actuality from bosh, our staunch doubt
wanting secretly to bleed and be washed.
We've inhabited discomfort, chiselled a routine out
of being too hot and nauseous from new food,
witnessed our bodies slicken up with pungent salt
like market olives in brine, until finally
this country is a truer fiction than home.
The mausoleums of its sultans mean something.
We find ourselves growing not impious,
asking questions of the silence
as if it were honestly there.
Is it wrong to watch and listen not
for concrete acts and words,
but arabesques of shape and sound?
What vanity is it that while there's extra money
in the bank, we are determined to rush
to see the occident the other way around?
Cobra charmers in the smoke of charring meat at dusk?

To gawk at the inadvertent psychedelia
of ancient tilework, and ask
might this impenetrable pattern not
mesmerize us into comprehension?
Must we always be condemned to smile
and smile across this cinematic gulf?

Certainly it would have been difficult,
if not impossible, to have imagined those storks,
white as labcoats, looking impassively
down from their jagged nests
atop the pillars of the Kasbah, at dusk.
(Everything here seems to happen at dusk.)
— Difficult to imagine, too, the wind
on that walk up the beach
past the men selling camel rides
to the eroded fortress. Blindingly scenic,
the endless sand whipping up in little storms.
— Imagine. We'd never seen riot police
in action before, phalanxed in flak and plexiglass,
beating back the rallied unemployed.
We half-ashamedly suspect
we're better people for having witnessed that.
— Yes, the journalistic thrill of witnessing
would have been impossible to conjure
by simply trolling the web for panoramic jpegs,
the weight of not having been there
cargoed in our hearts
like a crate of pomegranates
awaiting unloading from an anchored ship.
— Like the difference between praying to a God
and hoping like crazy one exists.
— The thrill we get from other people's faith
defines "vicarious," "parasitic," "bittersweet."
The judgement we almost pass on ourselves
in the silence after every Adhan,
if transcribed, might serve to reassure
the tourist of the future wracked with doubt:

It isn't lack of imagination that makes you come
to unimaginable places, instead of staying home.
Nor does the simple fact that you do not belong
entice you here, like children to forbidden rooms.

However much your interloping may feel wrong
(the misery of others doesn't make you strong),
there's cruelty too in the coziness of home:
it tricks us into thinking life is long.

9. *On Togetherness*

Togetherness means I want you alone,
to be there when you're really by yourself,
to really be myself when I'm alone.

The benefits of love are widely known,
but solitude contributes much to mental health.
Togetherness means I want you alone.

You'll likely greet this poem with a groan,
as though it constitutes an act of stealth.
But I just want to be myself when I'm alone.

By whom I do not mean the chump I loan
to dinner parties and affairs of wealth,
but the one who keeps it all together when alone.

I want to make myself a man of stone,
animated by the breath of love itself:
the solid Me you hope I am when I'm alone.

With you I sought a definition of my own,
and finally I know just what the hell
togetherness means: I want myself alone.
I want us both to be myself when I'm alone.

10. *Epilogue: In Praise of Staying Put*

Whether it means sitting cross-legged in a soyfield
serenely toying with the unsolvable mystery
of why right now rather than yesterday,
or sprawling undrunk on a bed heaped with coats,
spacing out as if the muffled joy below the floor
was going on tomorrow night instead,
I want to master it before I have no choice.

Maybe fortune falls more readily on the motion-
less than most of us act like we know,
invisibly descending like an ashen dust
left over from the magical explosion that began
the chase of life on Earth: the compulsive rush
to otherness the optimists call love,
preventing us from letting dust be dust

and settle down on us. Today the clouds are not
encouragingly plump and full of gusto,
nor is the late summer wind anything but hot,
nor the sun even visible beyond
a generalized white beaming not unlike
what some say we see in the moments after life
withdraws its motions. So why not

behave as though we're fated to the common plot
of birth, pursuit, failure, acceptance, and death,
and start preparing now for future letdowns,
refusing to look too closely within,
to track the satisfied desire to its source,
the heart-shaped kiln where mortal clay is fired
into vases too hot to keep flowers alive in.

Let us entertain the thought that happiness itself
is bleeding us like a leech applied by quacks
to cure an ache too deep for treatment,
not what the pessimists name "the human condition"
but something just as common to insects,
a twitching in the limbs left unmoving too long,
a sense of matter's hard helplessness in space:

the gene-charged embryos from which we grow,
the squishy fist that gets our blood to flow,
the skull-encased mush containing everything we know
and fear, the fragilities that make us go.

OVUM

Close your eyes, see
if you can find her mouth
before the yolk breaks. Proof,
sings desire's tremolo, lies in this
blind game of cradled egg
(though which outcome
proves what, and against whose palate
or irrepressible teeth
should the tiny yellow cosmos
finally burst, and after how many
preternaturally gentle passes
between your mouths?) but the longer both
song and yolk remain unbroken, the closer
comes the fervid pitch of one
to bringing on the spasm that will burst
the other. Proof,
if required, will swoop in like a dragon,
breathing something more fierce
than the fire you imagine: her still-shut eyes,
she trusts. You swallow.

WHAT LITTLE HISTORY

What little history the bedroom held
didn't matter. We were too busy to remember
how our building was once a ginger ale plant,

to think of anything but the bed, the ceiling,
us and then. I must be ovulating,
you said, interrupting, I just felt you

graze the top of me. Knowledge of anatomy
shaky, I tried to picture your insides as I'd seen them
diagrammed in textbooks,

but only a vaguely taurine silhouette
(uterus face, fallopian horns)
came to mind. Not your body or any woman's

but a Platonic blueprint, as distant from pleasure
as the ever-possible child was
from our thoughts. While together

we smoothed away biology's edges,
alone we remained discrete as ever
two people were, left to ponder such marvels

as the rising and lowering, dilation and closure
of your cervix, the mark on the ceiling
that might be a spider, the smiling menace

inside me: the part convinced
that if the condom ever broke and spilled its contents,
the consequences couldn't not be beautiful.

VOLTA

People wanted to call this electricity animal electricity...
But these people were wrong, given that the living or dead
creature contributes nothing to this electricity, which is not
connected to any vital function, since produced by merely
rubbing hairs, silk, wool, and even underwear.
—*Alessandro Volta, 1792*

Some nights just watching the lightning's not enough:
the window flickers white-hot as we lie
regaining our lungs, feeling vaguely nonplussed
at proving unequal to the storm outside.
Soon the warm inches between us shrink
to a lycra-tight heat, and with a sigh you rise,
restless with safety and hungry to think
there's more to fear than just the typical surprise
of outage or surge.
                                        (Phase back to the Age
of Reason: when Galvani hung frogs
by their spines from brass hooks, then
nudged their open nerves with iron rods,
he mistook their legs' resultant twitching
for proof of a ghostly current that coursed,
lightning-tongued, the length of their spas-
modic husks. He misnamed this force
"animal electricity," and decades bolted by
before a fellow countryman could show
the flow came not from the bodies at all,
but from the joining of unlike metals
in the moist environs even lifeless flesh left
to science. Ergo, the body electric only
borrows us.)
                                    But the hope of getting struck,
you know, is not to be chosen. Although the bolt
would brand you as a hazard-bride of luck,
kissed from on high, the hissing megavolts
of afterglow might leave you numb to us,
your whole body buzzing with tinnitus.

39

PRENUPTIALS

I.

In long blue rooms sequestered off
by portable walls, our lives are drawn for analysis

in vials of stoppered pulses. *Don't let them
take too much*, you quipped. But less the taking

it's the glimpse, the red flash as the nurse turns away
that whispers: love isn't limitless.

2.

Nor does it prick without compunction. When it comes
your turn, I muster every ounce of *sang-froid*

my relict reptilian brain-stem affords, and force
myself aversionless as the tourniquet

purples your vein for puncture. Your nails barely
plum my palm's cushion as the tip pushes

3.

and the beaker drinks. Four pink crescents flouresce
and fade, blood moons antiseptically eclipsed.

With our new thresholds freshly cottoned shut,
we reconfirm our names at the reception desk

and exit, two fewer tests left to take,
prepared to wait our lives for the results.

ON SITTING THROUGH *THE RITE OF SPRING*

The furor, dead for over ninety years
now seems masturbatory, hordes at the ballet
jerking taut decorum's futile leash,
believing they know they ought
to think it vile — the offered girl dancing herself
to dying — hot in their disgust as estrus dogs.

                            All those virgins' brittle
thrustings gird the sacred hill, under watch of elders salivating
at what they tell themselves is children's saintly bliss
but know damn well is knowledge. Insatiate
youth, if growing up won't outright pervert you
the pangs of nostalgia afterward might
someday find you longing for an altar
and a fire, and a knife, and a want
and a like-minded crew to dance naked with.

                            The primitive, they say
is one of our persistent fascinations, but it's the lingering taint
of our great-great-grandparents' indignation
that's brought us here; not Igor's martial erotics
or the gender-bending dancers, but this wish we harbour
to feel the shock the dead felt. Yes, the kettledrums
stir our hearts, the trumpets the nubs of our spines
and all that flaunted skin our sexes, but none of this
is new.
        We've gotten used to
not disappointment, but the sudden spikes
and dives of endless brief arousals. Tunes and beauties,
popcorn and other people's orgasms, the icy commonplace
that kids are cutest when they're not yours. If ever
concert halls were venues of escape, not today.
That old couple a row ahead of us, smooching
with tongues.
              How red our young discomfort.

GENERATION

Thank goodness for the blood,
for that affirmative pat on the head
from the universe: "You're still young,
you might skirt this yet another turn."

For soon enough, at the sight of a sandbox
a watery longing will surge up,
and out will gurgle the first words
of a brand new amphibian:

"I can't wait to meet our children."

Till then, let's keep our four collective feet
firm in this era of arid carelessness,
upon this rootless sand let us bask
like giants, levelling castles

we ourselves have just erected,
because we can't yet bear to let them stand.

QUESTIONS IN BED

Why must our minds tilt with our bodies,
horizonward? Will you ever stop

desiring me more than sleep? Honestly,
how low must my breathing sink

before you rouse yourself to check my pulse? Wrist,
or throat? Of course I'm serious —

who knows what brinks these unconscious hours
might drive us to, what precipice

that black limousine might glide serenely over,
tinted windows eyelids

blinding us to fast approaching bottom?
Is sex what pillows that ravine

and if so, what of love? I often wonder —
when our hands brush in this oblivion of down,

do our dreams converge? Is each of us kissed
by a promptly vanishing stranger,

an agent of the doubts that shame
our dailiness, becoming unabashed as we drift

apart on separate straits of zees? Which bits
of my you and your me are just figments

of this single-letter alphabet? How much brained-up
junk do we mistake for discovery?

THE BLIND VOYEUR

There I stood expecting cosmos
to flourish around my boots. But the gaps
in the cobblestone walk let gasp nothing
but loam. While pink-headed clubgoers
cliqued in glitter and sandalwood
scented the night themselfish, I leaned
back on the sidewalk gate, craning to glimpse
your black double through the drapes.

The woman you dubbed fashionista—
and everyone else dubbed Venus herself—
had sashayed her eyeshadowed way, at last
into my hours asleep. Abstraction
acted the spanish fly, I couldn't wait
till bedtime, when her vague soft
body would take shape from the onyx
ponds behind my eyelids.

A sort of pallor washed out
my daylights, you probably saw how
hollow you came to seem, as though the spectre
in the round asylum of my pupil as we fought
was not just your tiny reflection.

Fashionista vanished at my approach.
My dreamlife, as usual, forgave me.
Under the window, the futility of this.
The garbagey taste of just waking up
lit on my tongue from the gutters, warning
this temptation to knock
ought to be resisted, only waiting
would show me your silhouette,
the woman I loved with my eyes shut.

WHAT SEPTEMBER SWALLOWS

Summer, yes—
but what else? In one long autumnal gulp
the green irreverence that accrues
over three months of the kind
of beaming lucidity

Blake etched
with such heliocentric conviction.
What delusion, to permit this regret
like frost to pale with frigid dust
your flushed athletic lips,

the redness
they tugged to my surfaces. As if the sun
were ever more completely revered: heat
beneath, between, within our
creatured bodies given over

to melt.
How orchidaceous lying glazed in sweat
can make us feel, like whole bodies of lolling
tongues, how open, but of course
we teeter over into wilt.

It snows
sometimes in September. And my disbelief
at these soon-white fields morphs to knowing this:
we the pursued are chasers
of weather, and like historians

our quarry
never fails to estrange us. Circling back to stalk
the year's first snowfall, summer's embers
still hissing in our hearts,
we convince ourselves

this is new —
and those first flakes, in landing, elate like a touch
we forgot we'd ever shivered under, fingers
      we thought long past, reaching
            back from future summers.

I. NATIONAL HOLIDAY MORNING

The city hall clock dongs eight. Fog—
an oddly guttural thing to call
mere vapour—still gauzes my view across
the boatless river. It's not coldness
or the old stone comfort of the government district
that lets me re-wilderness the distant bank,
foresting away the neighbourhoods
of sallower children and gutters thronged
with earwigs and shingle chunks
mudding into rot.

Erasing the river's wrong side
is a matter for me not of condescension
but of civic love. Sometimes equality
must be invented, poverty dreamed gone—
just ask John Lennon. But don't imagine
such sightless visions as anything
beyond the flaccid standard, flags
over windless monuments. The only prophets here
are starlings, feeding from the sand
at the feet of the elms on the lawn
of the Justice Building. And grackles,
peering down from those selfsame trees
with jaundiced eyes, their heads tricked out
with iridescence.

Essentially we seek, though
not concertedly, a beacon. This
the wishful patriot in my gut is keen
to ulcerate himself with swallowed choler
to maintain. The vapours he refluxes up
condense to clouds, sugar-spun,
my just-woken head all too happily
nuzzles into. I allow myself the fantasy
that later, gathered at fogless twilight,

standing in brotherly clumps
as neutered gunpowder blooms
stemless flowers, we will wow
at the sky's defencelessness:
at the lightlessness of even everywhere
and nowhere, until you explode it.

II. NATIONAL HOLIDAY, MORNING AFTER

The rain held back
till the baited silence after
the bang the crowd
didn't yet know
meant the end. As the last
few harmless sparks
fizzled into the river,
the first mute drops nudged us
      as officers might
into dispersal.

If peopled rooms leave
the streets peaceful, must violence,
then, move indoors?
We two have slept together
many consecutive nights,
some torrid, many
like last, placid, backdropped
      by the nightlong
diminuendo of rain...

Sleep chosen, we valued
the weather's help in drowning out
the shouts in the street —
What ruckus? Each other
over others. We first touched
tongues in a thundershower, lunged
in the soak till our clothes clung,
      so now the storm belongs
to us, sex is exclusive, fair is fair and
carnival carnival — and you can save that
for the hooligans.

When morning rises up
to dry and dispossess us, I wander out
to brace myself with coffee
and idly scan for marks
of aftermath. The thin spent cylinder
of a lit-off firework juts up
from the damp grass by the river,
    a standing reminder
of how the celebration contrived
to lampoon our privacy, booming the dark
with those dazzling vows.

BEDROOM COMMUTE

Our bumpers kiss the coming wind like narcissists,
charging auto-erotically into ever-imminent
arrival. We can never get there as we were

before ignition, when the engine keyed our minds
to distance and defence, and the rest became
mere tribulation, hazy steel-floes

on grey seas home. The paved glide makes
the transformation smooth: by the time we reach
the city's fallow southern fringe, we've slipped free,

fishskinned from the workday's grip, exorcized
the sallow ghost of stress in smears of palm-sweat
that glisten on the wheel, evaporate.

A new looseness illumines our rearview eyes,
as though an angel's fumed in behind them,
possessed our templed brains for the truer cause

of leisure. Ours no longer the office of boss
and staffer, the grind of coffee and doorjamb smiles,
the being statuesque without

the admiration. We are most ourselves
when we're only almost home: when every taint
of the mechanical has vanished

from our conversation, and even the car
seems to be driving itself, as if animal
ensoulment came standard like cruise control.

It's only then that we forget tomorrow,
which at all other times except on weekends
dilutes the savour of our meals and dreams

with its insipid maybes. Once we pull up
the lane of our country haven that's become
eighty-percent bedroom—and not in the way

you want to think—something saddles us
again. We become the ridden, the burden-beasts
spurred to sleep toward the briefest of sunsets.

GESUNDHEIT

Convulsed by nose-gust in a dustless chrome box,
going down. Though alone, my thoughts still flirt
with contagion, the coming elevator-spread
pandemic, the spores that even now may wait,
barely dormant, amid the stack of oldish books
I grip — some Martian poets rarely looked at
anymore — their yellowed margins smelling
saccharine after decades of quarantine.

A hypochondriacal twinge. Who read these books,
rode this box before? I spray another clutch
of germ-bombs into the regurgitated air
and bless myself in biblio-whispered Deutsche,
sausage-tongued and unvoiced from having spent
the day with books instead of friends. Ploddingly
a blip of red-lit digits counts me down to one:

a vacant *bing* announces the reinstatement

of gravity. Faced with the half-serious choice
between self-checkout machine and carbon-based
librarian, I gravitate toward the quicker queue,
swayed by the clock's opinionless authority,
passive as its eyeless face ticks off another victory
for robots and their jerky ilk. Just two hands
and one field of view may prove a shame for us.

The foyer's all fluster and flux, a slow tornado
of revolving doors and the chiropractic clack
of turnstiles, the season buoying borrowers in
on gusts of ownerless wind. I sneeze again,
and hearing nothing in the wake, wonder which
among these fellow brains chimed an automatic
silent blessing in an alien tongue, a tic
symptomatic of a kind virus, its host sick

with wishing for that part of us that might escape.

IN EMERGENCY

The waiting room is redolent of cutbacks;
the pleather seats seethe with sweaty people
sentried-over by a muted TV
on a swivel, hung in a purgatorial
hush like a misplaced, punctuation mark,
the paper numbers we clutch all damp
and dull pauses in our non-cardiac,

imaginary hearts. Our real pulses
lurch and loll the durance of our stay here,
unregular as thunder in snow. Lungs alert
with hope of sigh and dread of gasp, we hover
like lucid dreamers crossed with insomniacs:
with Xs for eyes and yet unusually awake
to the imbalance sleep helps sheet over,

the surplus of us versus a deficit of breath.

AT THE DRONE RECITAL

The altar, laden with alert machines,
blinks and blinks. Everything does not appear
to be in holy order: pews sardined
with half-believers come to seek not light
but a dim hum to vanish into,
a vacuum-hour of escape
down an ambient sound-hole.
Midweek nights the chapel hosts
performers of its own slow dusk, elegists
as unwitting and innocent of sacrilege
as sound itself. Two young men drift onstage
like the grown ghosts of past choirboys
and install themselves amidst a Golgotha of gear:
laptops and soundboards flashing stop and go,
old hollow-bodies, violins, a mellotron,
a squeeze-box, castanets, a moog — plus
scads of DIY noisemakers: blocks of wood
to clop like the satyr's cloven hoof,
a Jew's harp fashioned of bamboo and brass,
a plastic ballpark clapper, two fry pans,
and closest to the sanctum's throat,
a defunct censer filled with cat's eyes
to be rattled and duly warped
with electronics. Astonishment awaits
the gap that will be left, what will go dumb
in us when silence vanishes.

Is that a twinge we feel of something nearing
wonder? How close it seems
to puzzlement. Drone drapes over us
like the shroud of some devotionless
yet powerful martyrdom: we've sacrificed
our yen for beat and melody
in the vague hope of audiencing
ourselves to some not-even divinity —

this sonic viscosity, tronic with unspecific
possibility. The noise the young men make
forgets us, for the one time we recall,
of what wishing is. Suddenly wanting's
rough-honeyed object cannot be made out,
and the smatterings of fact once not
susceptible to doubt just sit here,
exactly up to their ears
in absence.

THE ZERO OR THE EGG

> Love (the word used in tennis for 'zero') is said to come from
> l'oeuf (French for 'the egg'), the shape of zero. However, the
> exact origin of the word is still a matter of debate among experts.
> —John Dennison Clarke, *Grand Slam: The Story of Tennis*

The match begins with balanced scores of love:
the players poise to hatch a win from eggs
of youthful joy, each willing love to grow
on his side to fifteen, thirty, forty, ideally
leaving the other with nothing but the love
he started with—that same strung force that led
them both to empty morning courts they filled
with hopperfuls of practice balls they served
until their racket-arms ached like losing
and their vision swam with neon blots. Love
alone cannot do any more than let them qualify,
is crucial as oxygen and water and yet,
in competition, pointless: having gotten them
to zero it stays there, the cast-off shell
from which each emerges into every game,
set to match talent, will, focus, fitness, luck—
to be the first to loosen the mutual yoke
that binds even the most final of opponents
across the rifting net they share, love to love.

FROM THE CAFÉ OCCIDENTAL

On the rim of a ceramic mug made in China
just drained of the last sip
of steeped hibiscus,

a sparrow alights. On the mug's side
is painted a magpie, downscaled
to fit, faded, cap feathers bereft

of ebony sheen, emerald tail stunted
and mossy, rich signal of call
kilned silent forever.

Strange, the drinker's twinge of sympathy at this
shrinkage, the sudden poignancy
of the bigger bird caged

in pigment. Meanwhile, the urban sparrow bathes
in the tangs of steam still wafting
from the hot bottom

of the empty mug. In the morning air
warmth and chill spar in tug, nibble—
preening mates. Shivers

raise birdflesh on human arms in weather
this crisp, but the drinker feels
as unlike the sparrow as ever,

watching its dun feathers ripple
in the thinning steam.
Magpies in China

omen joy, their chitters good fortune. *But not
here*, thinks the drinker, who wonders
at Chinese hands cramping

to emboss empty mugs with birds of dubious
significance to foreigners, skewed
of scale, perchless, unheard.

Who at the sparrow too can't help but wonder,
as its barbed and delicate feet
clutch the dusky rim

just above the magpie's crown.
How it doesn't recognize
the picture as kin.

REHEARSAL

Now and then, too comfortable in living,
I envision the funerals to come. Nervous roomfuls
of people who've never seen me weep
attending my grief like wary zookeepers.

May they marvel not at my strong heart
and rationality, but at the animal
in my devastation. May my body pay salt
enough to fill hourglasses to last out

the lost days that should have been ours. I'm afraid,

however, that this tolerance I cultivate
like a medicinal mould inoculates
too well against sorrow. That when they're gone
I won't come through with the right kind of rage.

The day might fall tomorrow. The call
or the cop at the door I'd meet with an *Oh*—
and nothing more. I bite my cheeks in fearing love
leaves first those with fewest tears.

DECEMBER IS AMONG US

for Ben Jones on his 80th birthday

I took a twilight wander after the year's
first blizzard, to cobble a song together out
of under-whispers and clipped air.

The knee-high banks between sidewalk
and street formed one long sculpted undisturbed
soft illusion of porcelain frosted

with swan-down. Up the block a dry quiet caught
my throat; I ungloved a hand and plunged it
into cold instantaneity of snow.

As I lifted the pinking fistful to my mouth
I doubted, for the first time I could recall,
the safety of ingesting it. In fact

I'd never thought of snow as something even to *be*
"ingested," never questioned till now
whether snow is eaten or drunk, never asked:

What if it's acid like rain in the '80s,
or clotted with oxides, basically car exhaust
condensed and lowered to a soft freeze?

Oddly this is when I thought of you, Ben,
found myself taking up the scales
of your untrivial mind to weigh the vanity

of my paranoia against the sin-
cerity of my concern. At the same time
I wondered with some shame what strange fears

you may have grown into, what certainties
the years have earned you free from. Is
my seriousness as silly as I suspect,

seen by the thicker light of experience?
Whether the winters have markedly warmed,
each feels less momentous, a shallower threat,

like the difference between treading slippingly
across an iced-over puddle, and tromping out
to a probably frozen lake's

inescapable middle. I both ate the snow
and watched myself eat it. Neither of me
came away sated. Having analyzed it meant

the slush left me refreshless, clenched
a thirst (or is it hunger?) I once again
was forced to admit I'd long given refuge to.

Will we regain our sense of being fallen?
This is less a theological question
than the rhetorical flail of one too young

for true perspective, one to whom the fate
of humankind seems apt to be decided
by a loaded die weighted to roll only ones

forever, the cycloptic eyes
of apocalypse. I hope you can laugh at this;
after so long of starting each new year

a day before the rest of us, having banked
those seventy-nine extra days of wisdomtime —
enough to dispense in generous instants

for decades — I hope you can accept yourself
being spoken to not just as elder,
mentor, father, but as someone born

in the shimmering calm between
celebrations. If this means you get folded in
among the holy, holly, and hurrah,

it also marks you as one we look to
to unclutter this season, to sound
amid the peals of ribbon and reaming bells

your note of clarity. Every late December
you welcome me at your door, your handshake
that of a gentleman scholar, but the warm look

more how I imagine the canny captain
of an arctic icebreaker might regard
an earnest young crewman of potential

but still with much to learn. I am learning
that winter itself is worth gathering for,
that we need its almost-painless blade

to wound us into renewal. Yes, *almost*:
for the end may be painless, but the best I know
are those less finished the longer they live.

                                        30 December 2010

PROVIDENTIAL PARK

1.

Dune evokes a declining place,
a straggler's warren: to supine
and bake in its shadeless lee.

2.

Danger, beach ahead: the sunshine
twins itself astray and digs sands
of ache under your earliest layers.

3.

Staycation Canadian, and be patient.
The crayfish rate may not outpace
the shade quotient, but wait for it

4.

instead in slow rays. Those were not the days
when coppertone-deafness meant
and kept on meaning, refusing to fade.

5.

White, and proudest when brown,
the majority perjures race war,
their voguish sun wishing us one colour.

6.

Lake ahoy. The blueful day makes a lure
of amber water. Above us the terns
turn without apparent pattern

7.

at the speed of magic. Chest-deep
and half a fathom out, the clans on shore
bask in iridescent splotches.

8.

Later, lacking birchbark, we resort
to kindling floormat jetsam:
Tim Hortons' cups and other scraps of upwash
that parody survival in their slow

9.

biodegradation. I am
Arcadian, entranced without doors.

10.

Up floors of spiritual awareness,
we sit minding the fire,
thinking it so much oranger than it is.

11.

Near midnight the lake's a slick eerie
of ink fringed with poison ivy,
millennia of unwritten polemics —

12.

The Great Chillax. As if
weekending suddenly becomes the black
to living's white.

WHAT'S AT HAND

I first learned numbers as fingers
proudly brandished at grownups, two splayed
hands making ten, the anatomic roots
of decimals unknowingly displayed.

Before it came to stand for peace
or victory, Baden Powell's cub salute
or even shadow-puppet bunny ears,
my fingered V evinced extremity of youth.

How soon our digits prove inadequate.
Eleven is the first challenge, and from there-
abouts the task becomes abstract, arithmetical:
to add it up without looking anywhere

but within. Now that I'm a finger away
from six hands of age, inquisitive children gape
as I flash ancestral palms at them
like a cornered laboratory ape.

Even empty hands hold evidence
of every passing year; while palmistry
plots expectancies in creases grasping deepens
I count on forgetting into mystery:

those moments, increasing in frequency,
when I stare down at the five-legged creatures
attached to my wrists. *Where am I?*
An ancient zero slips across my features.

QUESTIONS IN BED

Is silence plausible? Could I describe
right now, for instance, amid the ambient hum

of myriad appliances, distant car noise
and my own inner whispering,

as truly silent? What of the assassin wind
drawing its incomparably long blade across

the hollow of the moon's throat? How long
have I mistook this lunacide for peace?

Even those country nights under riddles
of pinprick stars: was that unpolluted

hush in which I basked actually the spheres
grinding at frequencies pitched above

the ear directly to the unreposing seat
of love and motion, a kind of high-

falutin booty-music? In calling dancing
"getting down," from what height do we envision

ourselves descending? Must the rugs up there remain
uncut? Is the total absence of sound perhaps

exactly as far beyond our grasp as paradise?
Does even snoring hymn

that dashed hope — the single log across
the hushing gully, sawn in half?

CARRION COMFORT

They innocently wish me dead:
  Muskoka'd supine and swallowed
into hot sleep just as they begin
    to turn, my left hand noose-dangling

limply to the planks, arrested mid-reach
    beside a tepid gin and tonic with three
lozenges of melted ice abob on top, three
    swirling water-clots that mirror the three

birds that wheel, agents of fortune, over my not-
    yet corpse. Torpid and blind, my head lolled
to one side and drooling, how possibly
    mortifying. If those I love could

hover over and watch my slackened
    body snore, how long could even
the motherly stare before my form became
    just that, a prone form and nothing more,

like a proper name droned
    into nonsense? The long view
from above the trees must reduce me
    to meat, a lump of nutrients

to be scavenged, lunch as imagined
    from the breakfast table, the delicious
tasteless future. The scenes I miss
    in helpless sleep become the inverse

of dreams, actual events that haunt by their very
    lack of vividness, my failure to stay
awake for them: the summer celebration
    going on inside, four generations

trading morsels with the kin they only see
    on holidays, snacking their way to feeling
safe with one another, showing teeth
    in laughter. The jokes they maybe make

at my oblivious expense, slapping tabletops
    or giddy knees, wondering out loud
when they should save me from the heat,
    or whether the encroaching shade will prove

enough. High above, the vultures turn
    counter-clockwise, mechanically
grinding off the breathless seconds left
    in the eleventh hour of their prey.

In habit's rapture they await a lack
    of motion, a stillness long enough
to drape their hungry hopes on,
    the confirmation of my anima's escape —

but then I wake. At once the sun
    unfogs my eyes and strikes my vision
white until my pupils shrink to pencil tips,
    and then the spires of pine-tops

and the raptor-dotted sky. Reactions
    tumble in my lusted-after blood:
surprise, morbid inner laughter
    at the thwarted blunderings of instinct,

whispers of fear, and finally the thrill,
    the shrill tingle in the limbs at being
hunted. Little but the actual stink
    of black feathers and a scimitar beak

aswim in my innards will ever purge
   these nerves' elation at the kinked
chambers of the animal brain, its thirst
   to kill without murder, its spark-lit

hatches and dark *Always*. I worry
   what my family will think when I emerge
out of the heat, dream-stunned and un-
   steady on my feet from having

drunk myself free of this dimension
   in the midday sun. Should I regale the cottageful
of them with my eviscerate visions,
   fables of the infinite small impalements

that await us at nature's unforked
   banquet plank? Will it just clang with bathos—
the sheer breadth of my escape? There's a fundament
   that can't be conveyed, a tint up there

each of us sees uniquely, a blue
   beyond blue, a life in the guts of death
that belongs to us. Perhaps it's best kept quiet.
   I greet my uncles' teasing with a smile,

and wash my hands to eat.

THE COCKTAIL GROWL

My stomach's threat resounds
with empty menace. *Or what?*

I drink you in, lacking anything
to wash down, so you repeat.

To vomit or converse: it's that
unclear to me. Zingers? Eros?

So much of our hunger is something else.

EULOGY FOR THE QUICK

and only partly caught. Not memories,
but traces of her flurried passing by my temple—glances
of skin, arcane scraps of fabric and scent, talk in heady snatches:

for these I am gathered here today,
mourning in anticipation. Hours ago and already
I can't keep straight whether hair sang red, or dress, or whether,

yes—neither—only my ears in the bloodrush.
And the perfume, it wasn't hers. That magnolia tree's
losing blossoms all over the sidewalk, every little fall loosing,

like a snuffed wick, a scent of expiration.
Maybe if I ran back down there now, some trigger, a sniff
of a shaft of light still dusted with her—but no, I must accept,

as the open ear accepts an unexpected whisper, she
is but a composite, best remembered by the one clipped
string I caught as she spoke into her tiny cell: *late, gotta go, yes, I'll call,*

THE FRESHLY MADE BED

It reclines in a pond of white light
cast down by the clouds,
concealing under quilt and pillows
pieces of its nighttime
occupants' bodies, microscopic evidence
of wellness and decline: flecks
of skin and wiry sprigs of hair —
not to mention dried excretions.

Precisely. The freshly made bed assuages
our dread of the unmentioned,
setting out a tidy front that never
hints at the decay within. Affix
the coffin's lid and tuck
the corners under, whistling out
the morning for what may always be

the final time. Dwindler,
never forget your bed's a chunk
of the eventual, a dense puff of heaven-breath,
the closest you might ever come
to afterlife. When you pull back the covers,
listen for the blast of distant trumpets.

APOCALYPTIST

I haven't wanted to be tilling sand
to grow stunted pulses for prison bread,
for gruel. Nor does my diet of legumes,
rice and roughage conceal a longing to tear,
dear auditors, your throats out with my teeth. Perish
the thought. As a parasite upon its host, I thrive
on your ignoring me while knowing,
by the devilled shafts of sunset angling
nightly through the bars of your mind's asylum,
I'm there. Like a staple gunned in
to an anaesthetized palm. What's that you feel?
A brutal nil: once quack Dr. Cole's done peddling his barely
entertaining pedantry, I'll sidle up to the MC
and book what he doesn't know will be
the last open mic slot of all times —

And what I utter when I take the stage will quickly make
lucid my lack of intention, my status as
a vehicle through which the fallen universe
rhapsodizes on the myriad
hues of its bruises. If only my mother's blue eyes!
…and so on. They'll no doubt think I'm losing
the proverbial *It*, which once they know
Bibilically enough to realize it's communist
in its doling out of earnestly tongued-
up-to climax, they'll find themselves pining
for the celibacy of gobbledegook.
And once they do that I'll starve their poverty,
blueball them with muzak and dumbphone pornography until
until until untilling leaves us all seedless —

ACKNOWLEDGEMENTS

Some of these poems appeared in *The Fiddlehead, Prism International,* and *Riddle Fence,* as well as in the chapbook *Sirens* (Cactus Press, 2011). My thanks to the editors of each.

The epigraph from John Ashbery on the dedication page is drawn from "Sleepers Awake," from his 1995 collection *Can You Hear, Bird.* The epigraph to "Chase Sequence: *8. The Answer of Travel"* is from Elizabeth Bishop's "Questions of Travel," the title poem of her 1965 collection. The epigraph to "Volta" is from a 1792 letter by Alessandro Volta, inventor of the battery, after whom the volt is named. The title of "Carrion Comfort" is lifted, with deep respect, from Gerard Manley Hopkins. I like to think he wouldn't have minded.

Particular debts of gratitude are owed to several of my friends and fellow poets: Ross Leckie, for his continual receptivity, guidance, and encouragement (with reservations at just the right times, especially early on); Brecken Hancock, for the intelligence and openness of her responses to my poems over the years, which has helped drive me to write better ones; Daniel Scott Tysdal, for his generosity and relentless creative force; Jim Johnstone, for his timely and crucial advocacy of my work; and my editor, James Langer, for his craftsman's capacity to inhabit and improve someone else's (often very stubborn) vision.

Thanks as well to all my other friends: you're behind this too. And to my family, for their truly unconditional support.

And finally to Pascale, without whom.

photo: Pascale McCullough Manning

Stewart Cole grew up in the Rideau Valley south of
Ottawa and has since lived in Victoria, Montreal, and
Fredericton. His poetry and reviews have appeared
in a variety of publications across Canada. His chap-
book *Sirens* was published by Cactus Press in 2011.
He now lives in Toronto.

Typeset in Adobe Fournier.
Printed on Zephyr Antique Laid by Coach House Printing.